B Sheeran Ed
Ed Sheeran

ED SHEERAN

SINGER & SONGWRITER

KATIE LAJINESS

Big Buddy Books
An Imprint of Abdo Publishing
abdopublishing.com

BIG BUDDY POP BIOGRAPHIES

abdopublishing.com

Published by Abdo Publishing, a division of ABDO, PO Box 398166, Minneapolis, Minnesota 55439.
Copyright © 2018 by Abdo Consulting Group, Inc. International copyrights reserved in all countries.
No part of this book may be reproduced in any form without written permission from the publisher.
Big Buddy Books™ is a trademark and logo of Abdo Publishing.

Printed in the United States of America, North Mankato, Minnesota.
092017
012018

Cover Photo: Charles Sykes/Invision/AP.
Interior Photos: Alex Huckle/Getty Images (p. 27); Dan Kitwood/Getty Images (p. 9); Jamie
    McCarthy/Getty Images (pp. 15, 29); John Phillips/Getty Images (pp. 5, 21); Kevork Djansezian/
    Getty Images (p. 23); Loccisano/Getty Images (p. 11); Mark Sagliocco/Getty Images (p. 19);
    Michael Samir Hussein/Getty Images (p. 13); Taylor Hill/Getty Images (p. 17); Theo Wargo/Getty
    Images (p. 25).

Coordinating Series Editor: Tamara L. Britton
Contributing Editor: Jill Roesler
Graphic Design: Jenny Christensen

Publisher's Cataloging-in-Publication Data

Names: Lajiness, Katie, author.
Title: Ed Sheeran / by Katie Lajiness.
Description: Minneapolis, Minnesota : Abdo Publishing, 2018. | Series: Big buddy pop biographies |
    Includes online resources and index.
Identifiers: LCCN 2017943906 | ISBN 9781532112188 (lib.bdg.) | ISBN 9781614799252 (ebook)
Subjects: LCSH: Sheeran, Ed, 1991-.--Juvenile literature. | Folk-rock music--Juvenile literature. |
    Guitar music (Rock)--Juvenile literature. | Great Britain--Juvenile literature.
Classification: DDC 782.42164092 [B]--dc23
LC record available at https://lccn.loc.gov/2017943906

CONTENTS

FAMOUS MUSICIAN

Ed Sheeran is an **award**-winning **musician**. His music is a mix of folk, **hip-hop**, and **pop**. After writing many hit songs, Ed has become one of today's most popular artists.

He has been in magazines. And, his music has been in movies. Ed has fans around the world!

SNAPSHOT

NAME:
Edward Christopher Sheeran

BIRTHDAY:
February 17, 1991

BIRTHPLACE:
Halifax, West Yorkshire, England

POPULAR ALBUMS:
÷, ×, +

FAMILY TIES

Edward Christopher Sheeran was born on February 17, 1991, in Halifax, England. His parents are Imogen and John Sheeran. Ed has an older brother named Matthew, who is also a singer.

DID YOU KNOW?
Growing up, Ed's family did not own a TV for many years. Instead, the family worked on creative projects.

WHERE IN THE WORLD?

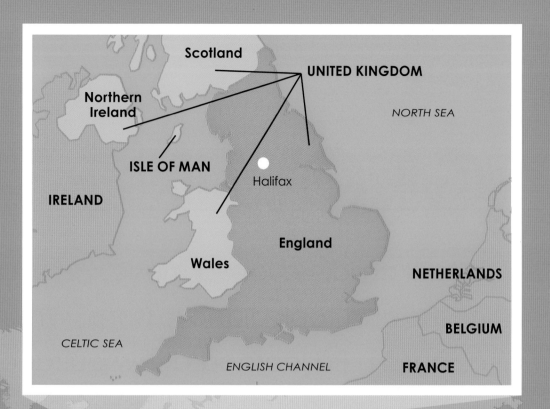

GROWING UP

As a child, Ed loved music. He sang in choirs and took piano lessons. When he was about 11, Ed learned a few guitar **chords**. It wasn't long before he was writing songs.

At first, Ed was afraid to **perform** in front of people. But he didn't give up. Soon, Ed felt comfortable onstage.

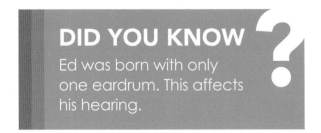

DID YOU KNOW

Ed was born with only one eardrum. This affects his hearing.

At age 12, Ed was in a band called Rusty. Sadly, the band only stayed together for about two months.

Growing up, Ed was bullied in school. Outside of school, he spent a lot of time making music. At age 13, Ed made his first independent album, *Spinning Man*. The next year, he **released** his first **EP**, *The Orange Room*.

When Ed was about 16, he left school and moved to London, England. He began taking classes at a school called Access to Music. There, he learned to be a better **musician**.

Kids teased Ed about his red hair and glasses. But Ed did not let bullies get him down.

STARTING OUT

Ed wanted to be a famous **musician**. From 2006 to 2009, he independently **released** three **EPs**.

Throughout 2009, Ed continued **performing** and recording music. That year, he played 312 shows! Ed made money by selling his music on the streets and after shows.

DID YOU KNOW
Ed's fans are known as Sheerios.

In 2009, Ed won a Battle of the Bands contest. As a prize, he made a deal to release his single "Let It Out."

To build upon his success, Ed moved to the United States in 2010. In Los Angeles, California, he met actor Jamie Foxx. Soon, Ed was recording in Jamie's **studio**.

In 2011, Ed **released** an **EP** called *No. 5 Collaborations Project*. It sold thousands of copies during the first week. And it reached number two on the iTunes chart. Soon, Ed had a record contract with Atlantic Records.

DID YOU KNOW?
As of 2017, Ed had released 13 EPs. Some songs were recorded at live events.

Ed opened for 66 of Taylor Swift's concerts during her 2013 *Red* tour.

BIG BREAK

Ed's first album, *+ (Plus)*, was a huge hit. More than 2 million copies sold in the United Kingdom. "The A Team" was on the *Billboard* charts for 26 weeks. It peaked at number 16.

In 2014, Ed **released** his second album, *x (Multiply)*. The music video for "Thinking Out Loud" has nearly 2 billion views on the website YouTube. It was the first song to have more than 500 million plays on Spotify.

In 2013, Ed sold out his first of three straight Madison Square Garden concerts in three minutes!

MIXING SOUNDS

As a talented songwriter, Ed has worked with many different **musicians**. Together with Pharrell Williams, Ed wrote "Sing" for his x (*Multiply*) album. In 2015, Ed **released** "Growing Up (Sloan's Song)" with **hip-hop** artists Macklemore & Ryan Lewis.

Ed wrote "Love Yourself" for Rihanna to sing. But, **pop** star Justin Bieber sang it instead.

Ed wrote "Moments," "Little Things," "Over Again," and "Summer Love" for One Direction.

Ed has written songs for movies. "I See Fire" played during the closing credits in *The Hobbit: Desolation of Smaug*.

He also wrote and **performed** the song "All of the Stars" for the 2014 movie *The Fault in Our Stars*.

DID YOU KNOW?

Ed launched his own record label. He named it Gingerbread Man after his red hair.

In 2015, Ed sold out three nights in a row at Wembley Stadium. The London stadium can hold 93,000 people.

AWARD SHOWS

Ed often attends **award** shows. There, he sometimes **performs** his latest song and wins awards. In 2013, Ed performed "Lego House" at the *Billboard* Music Awards.

"The A Team" won the 2012 Ivor Novello Music Award for Best Song Musically and Lyrically. He also accepted the 2013 Teen Choice Award for Choice Music Breakout Artist.

"Thinking Out Loud" won the 2016 Grammy Award for Song of the Year.

GIVING BACK

Ed has spent a lot of time and money to help others. He participated in Red Nose Day. This group helps to fight illness and **promote** education. Ed also played concerts in Ireland to raise money for teenagers with **cancer**.

Ed traveled to Liberia to help homeless children for the Red Nose Day cause.

OFF THE STAGE

In 2015, Ed hurt himself while jumping off a boat. So, he had **surgery** to fix his broken eardrum. Then Ed took a year off to spend time with his friends and family. He went on many adventures, such as swimming with sharks and bungee jumping.

Ed traveled to Iceland and Japan during his year off.

BUZZ

Ed has become one of the most popular **musicians** in the world. In 2017, he **released** his third album, *÷ (Divide)*. In less than three weeks, it sold 500,000 copies in the United States! Ed's fans are excited to see what he does next!

DID YOU KNOW?
In March 2017, Ed kicked off another world tour.

Ed sang on *TODAY* in New York City, New York. Fans arrived hours early for a chance to see him perform.

GLOSSARY

award something that is given in recognition of good work or a good act.

cancer any of a group of very harmful diseases that cause a body's cells to become unhealthy.

chord three or more musical tones sounded at the same time.

EP extended play. A music recording with more than one song, but fewer than a full album.

hip-hop a form of popular music that features rhyme, spoken words, and electronic sounds. It is similar to rap music.

musician someone who writes, sings, or plays music.

perform to do something in front of an audience. A performance is the act of doing something, such as singing or acting, in front of an audience.

pop relating to popular music.

promote to help something become known.

release to make available to the public.

studio a place where music is recorded.

surgery (SUHRJ-ree) the treating of sickness or injury by cutting into and repairing body parts.

To learn more about Ed Sheeran, visit **abdobooklinks.com**.
These links are routinely monitored and updated to provide
the most current information available.

31

INDEX